FOUR KINDS OF

CHRISTMAS

WHICH ARE YOU?

FOUR KINDS OF

CHRISTMAS

WHICH ARE YOU?

GLEN SCRIVENER

10 Publishing
a division of 10 of those.com

Copyright © 2015 by Glen Scrivener

First published in Great Britain in 2015

Reprinted 2016

British Library Cataloguing in Publication Data
A record for this book is available from the British Library

ISBN: 978-1-910587-45-4

Designed and typeset by Pete Barnsley (Creative Hoot)

Printed and bound by Nørhaven

10Publishing, a division of 10ofthose.com
Unit C, Tomlinson Road, Leyland, PR25 2DY, England

Email: info@10ofthose.com
Website: www.10ofthose.com

CONTENTS

MY KIND OF CHRISTMAS

Every kid wakes early for Christmas, but I woke with the sunshine blazing through the curtains. Christmas is, after all, one of the longest days of the year. In Australia anyway.

Breakfast was a sickly mix of tropical fruit and Cadbury's Roses. Having coated my face in a mango-chocolate glaze, I'd pull on my Sunday best – a surfer T-shirt / board shorts combo (*ironed* for special occasions) – and we'd head to church.

Afterwards it was presents and then lunch. Usually some kind of roast. Not turkey, of course. No one chooses turkey unless compelled by centuries of peculiar tradition. Freed from the constraints of custom, Australians are able to see turkey for what it is: the food equivalent of a dehumidifier, sucking the moisture out of every cell in your body. Most Australians have ditched turkey since it has all the texture – but none of the flavour – of cotton wool.

Of course, having rid ourselves of turkey, the

whole traditional Christmas lunch then falls apart. Soon you realise that every other component had only been drafted in to make the bird edible. Gravy *and* stuffing *and* cranberry sauce *and* bread sauce – bread sauce! – all exist merely to wash down this Death Valley made flesh. In the old world, Brussels sprouts – those fetid parcels of chewy methane – can almost be justified for their moisture content. Lose the turkey, though, and it's a whole new world of possibilities.

So for lunch we would have lamb, or beef, or seafood, or a barbecue, or anything but turkey. We would pull our crackers, don our paper crowns, tell terrible jokes and eat till we burst. Then burst we did, outside for a swim, before hours of backyard cricket and finally a classic Australian carol:

Jingle bells, jingle bells,
Jingle all the way,
Christmas in Australia
On a scorching summer's day.
Jingle bells, jingle bells,
Christmas time is beaut.
Oh what fun it is to ride
In a rusty Holden ute.[1]

Standard stuff really. Unless you're a Brit, in which case you're recoiling violently from the page, howling, 'Wrong! Make him stop! He's ruining Christmas!' I'm guessing that's your reaction because, having lived half my life in the UK, I've learnt the limits of British tolerance.

You Brits are an understanding bunch – perhaps the most tolerant in the world. You manage to forgive so much: *Neighbours* (remember Bouncer's dream sequence?), The Wiggles, Dannii Minogue (once again, we're sorry, please accept Kylie as a peace offering). Yes, Britons will forgive a lot, but one thing the Brits seem to find inconceivable is a summer Christmas.

And you know what? I think you might be on to something. Blazing sunshine is not the right context for Christmas. Proper Christmas happens 'in the bleak midwinter'.

CHRISTMAS IN THE DARK

I'm not just saying this to regain the favour of turkey-loving Britain. I'm genuinely convinced on this one: Christmas is a winter celebration. I don't really mean the weather. I do mean the mood. Whatever the hemisphere, whatever the climate, there is something inescapably wintry about Christmas – at least, according to the Bible.

In this book we're going to explore a famous Christmas reading – it gets wheeled out at all the traditional carols services, it is sung (twice!) during Handel's *Messiah*, and it predicts the birth of Jesus 700 years ahead of time. Here's the place of Christmas according to the Old Testament prophet Isaiah:

> *The people walking in darkness*
> *have seen a great light;*
> *on those living in the land of deep darkness*
> *a light has dawned.*

— Isaiah 9:2

Christmas begins in darkness. Isaiah mentions it twice in one sentence – the second time he calls it 'deep' darkness. Yes, a light dawns but, as we'll see, it comes from out of this world. Darkness is the context.

The rest of the Bible agrees. Eavesdrop, even briefly, on a carol service and you'll hear repeated references to darkness. The popular Bible readings are full of darkness imagery. In the original telling of the story, Christmas happens with people huddling together in the gloom. It's not about reflecting the brightness of our sunny circumstances. Christmas, according to the Bible, belongs in a land of deep shadow.

That's important to remember at Christmas, especially because it can be such a difficult time. If you're ill, unemployed, broke, single, divorced, depressed or in any other way transgressing Our Festive Expectations, Christmas can be really rough. In a 2010 survey 18% of respondents agreed with the statement 'I dread Christmas'.[2] In another survey it was revealed that 19% 'hate' Christmas parties.[3] For many of us, Christmas is anything but the most wonderful time of the year. Every relational fracture is exacerbated, every family breakdown is exposed and every pang of bereavement is given fresh oxygen. Half a million UK families will have an empty chair at Christmas lunch because they've lost someone this year. Christmas doesn't seem to help at these times but only to hurt.

If you are finding Christmas particularly hard, Isaiah assures you: you're not alone. The true context for Christmas is darkness. But what do we do about it?

FOUR KINDS OF CHRISTMAS

This book is about four responses to the darkness. We're exploring four kinds of Christmas, but each kind of Christmas represents an approach to life too – a way of handling the brokenness of this world.

1. SCROOGE

A Scrooge says, 'Yes, darkness is all around. And it always will be. Act accordingly.'

2. SHOPPER

A Shopper says, 'The light is going out so let's celebrate while we can.'

3. SANTA

A Santa says, 'Darkness? What darkness?' They choose to believe that all is light.

4. STABLE

The Stable preaches the original Christmas message. Here we take the darkness seriously, but by entering it we are offered the brightest future.

The four kinds of Christmas illustrate four ways that we handle the struggles of life. Which do you lean towards? You can always take the test at www.fourkindsofchristmas.com and find out.

On one level, all this is just a bit of fun. On another, there's nothing more serious. Really we're asking the big questions: what is the world really like? Where are we headed? And how should we live in response? The four kinds of Christmas are four approaches to life, and as we go through them I'd love you to be thinking: which am I? Which do I want to be? And what *is* the best approach to the darkness?

Let's begin with someone right at home in the darkness ...

1. SCROOGE

'Darkness is cheap,' observed Charles Dickens in *A Christmas Carol*, 'and Scrooge liked it.' Ebenezer Scrooge had a ruthlessly consistent approach to the darkness. He looked out on a bleak world, looked ahead to a bleak future and lived accordingly. Listen as he spreads his own brand of Christmas cheer: 'Every idiot who goes about with "Merry Christmas" on his lips should be boiled with his own pudding, and buried with a stake of holly through his heart.' Dickens depicts a man thoroughly adapted to the dark: 'External heat and cold had little influence on Scrooge. No warmth could warm, no wintry weather chill him.

No wind that blew was bitterer than he, no falling snow was more intent upon its purpose, no pelting rain less open to entreaty.'

Here is one way of handling the darkness: make your home in it. Become just as bitter as your bitter circumstances and say, 'Bah! Humbug!' to Christmas. That's an approach to Christmas, and it's an approach to life. Do you know Scrooges? Are you a Scrooge?

I am. A bit. Alright, I can be a lot of a Scrooge at times. If I'm honest, the darkness is not just 'out there', in my wintry circumstances. It's also 'in here', in my heart. When life gets hard, I get harder. When things turn gloomy, so do I. And when the lights come on, I'm not always that keen to brave the brightness.

Every nightclub owner knows this. How do they get rid of their punters at closing time? How do they end the mystique which would otherwise lock burgeoning lovebirds in a doe-eyed embrace forever? Simple. Turn on the lights. Pimples, wrinkles and bloodshot eyes are all lit up and the romance is killed instantly. In the darkness it's easy to pretend. In the light our true selves – warts and all – become known. And, as T.S. Eliot wrote,

'Humanity cannot bear very much reality.'[4]

What if God is a dazzling source of light and life? This is how the Bible describes him. And what if he's calling you on to the dance floor, calling you to draw near? How do you react?

If you're anything like me, your knee-jerk response is to shrink back and hide in the shadows. In the dark we can do what we want. In the gloom we won't be bothered, or shown up, or held to account. That's why the darkness doesn't just happen to us. We also choose it.

Do you ever wonder why Christmas can be so strained at times? We are surrounded by the people we love the most and yet they are the ones we speak to *most* harshly. We reserve our worst behaviour, our bitterest words, our ugliest selfishness for those we call our 'loved ones'. What are we like? If you ask me, there's not only darkness around us in our suffering circumstances; there's also darkness within us in our selfish hearts.

And if this isn't bad enough, Isaiah points out the deepest kind of darkness – the darkness of death. The old King James translation puts it memorably. We are: 'they that dwell in the land of the shadow of death' (Isaiah 9:2). That's our situation. Mount Doom towers over us, overshadowing all we do. This creeping oblivion – death – will claim us all. And Merry Christmas to you and yours!

Yes, I know, this is a bit 'Bah! Humbug!' right now. But that's the point. As with *A Christmas Carol*, the best stories begin with a problem. And according to the Bible, this is ours – we're in a pit, groping in the dark. There's an incredible happy ending, I promise, but right now we need to face facts.

What do you think? Is there any truth to this? Is darkness a fair summary of our human problem? If so, what's a good response? Probably none of us want to follow Scrooge. So what about a more popular kind of Christmas ...

2. SHOPPER

If Scrooge believes it's darkness now and darkness forever, the Shopper says, 'Don't be so gloomy! Stoke the fires, let's celebrate!' The Christmas Shopper wears the gaudiest seasonal knitwear, the novelty reindeer socks and the mistletoe headband. They raise their glasses of festive refreshments and wish everyone 'A Very Happy Winter.' The Shopper is not religious – they've given up on Jesus and church (along with Father Christmas and fairy stories). Without such beliefs they figure that this life is all there is, so they try to make the most of it. 'Eat, drink and be merry for tomorrow we die' is their unofficial motto.

Shoppers are not necessarily consumerists (though they are susceptible to that trap). Essentially they are merrymakers. They spend big, rug-up warm and live it up while they can.

There's something right about the Shopper response. We're not meant to be Scrooges. We were built for joy.

The prophet Isaiah – whose words we looked at earlier – goes on to speak of the future that the Christmas Child will bring. Here's what Isaiah is looking forward to at the end of all things:

You have enlarged the nation
    and increased their joy;
they rejoice before you
    as people rejoice at the harvest,
as warriors rejoice
    when dividing the plunder.

— Isaiah 9:3

How does Isaiah think of the future? With 'joy'. The word 'rejoice' is used three times in one sentence. And our future will be all the more joyous for having come *through* the darkness. On the far side of this dark valley, Isaiah looks forward to an incredible hope – liberation and world peace:

> *For as in the day of Midian's defeat,*
> *you have shattered*
> *the yoke that burdens them,*
> *the bar across their shoulders,*
> *the rod of their oppressor.*
> *Every warrior's boot used in battle*
> *and every garment rolled in blood*
> *will be destined for burning,*
> *will be fuel for the fire.*

— Isaiah 9:4–5

Picture the scene Isaiah is painting. All weapons are melted down and turned into tractors, televisions and toasters. Blood-stained military uniforms are no longer needed. John Lennon might have *sung* '*Happy Xmas (War is Over)*' but Isaiah *promised* it. There will be a time when warfare ceases and the whole world will gather around a great bonfire to celebrate.

Right now we live amidst darkness, defeat, burdens and battle. Right now we suffer through war and bloodshed. But the Christmas Child will bring an end to war. He will prove to be a Prince of Peace.

And when he ushers in that joyful future, it will be a time of feasting and celebration. In fact it will be a lot like Christmas.

Every time Jesus describes his future hope, he speaks of it in terms of a family gathering around great food, with friendship, singing and celebrations. According to Jesus, creation is heading towards feasting joy. And so the Christmas Shoppers are right to emphasise family, food and festivities. Such celebrations reflect a deep truth about what we were created for. But there's a problem.

If you're a Shopper, you don't actually believe in the happily-ever-after. Essentially a Shopper has the same view of the future as Scrooge. Without a belief in God or anything beyond death, the Shopper's life is all about blazing brightly now because the grave awaits. And when the big day is over, when the batteries have died, the tree has withered and the credit card bills hit the doormat, the valley of the shadow remains.

If we want a meaningful and joyful Christmas, a true hope for the future is vital. Without such hope, Christmas cheer is like tinsel and we are like the tree – we are perishing. We can surround ourselves with family, feasting and festivities, but those things cannot keep us alive. We can decorate ourselves with the baubles of earthly success, but nothing can stop the rot. Without God we have no life in us – no *real* life that can possibly outshine the shadow of death.

So what should we do? Get depressed and become Scrooges? Or maybe we should just pretend the darkness away. That's what the Santas do ...

3. SANTA

The Scrooges and the Shoppers of this world are pretty secular. They're not really 'believers'. The Santas of this world are different. They are spiritual – trusting that there's more to life than this valley of deep shadow. Unlike the Scrooges and the Shoppers, the Santas *believe*.

What do they believe?

Essentially they believe in Santa. They don't imagine there's a fat man living at the North Pole, rather they think there *is* a God (or some kind of spiritual power) and he's basically a big Santa in the sky.

The similarities between Santa and popular perceptions of God are endless. As I describe Santa, you'll see how much it sounds like God-talk – or at least, the God-talk of many:

Santa is basically for children. He lives very far away. He's irrelevant to the vast majority of our lives, but if we really want something, we might put in a request. He doesn't ever show up – not that we see. But actually we're not sure we want him to show up. We want what Santa gives us, but we'd rather he didn't pull up a chair and share our pudding. We're probably glad that Santa never makes an appearance during the festivities. Frankly I'm nervous about what the old man might say after a couple of glasses of red wine. He may give a jolly 'ho, ho, ho', but push beneath the beard and the catchphrase and I'm just not sure what's there.

That's Santa. But it's also a common view of God. For so many people God is a distant, mostly irrelevant, possibly jolly but not particularly personable dispenser of *stuff*. We want his things. We certainly don't want him. And isn't it curious the way Santa gives better gifts to the rich kids? Very suspect. That's our complaint against Santa *and* against God. We question his fairness, and beneath the propaganda we wonder, 'Is he *really* all-loving like the stories say?'

According to the mythology Santa is generous, giving gifts to all the children of the world. But Santa doesn't give gifts, does he? He gives rewards for good behaviour. And if you're naughty, you get coal in your stocking.

A friend of mine was six years old when her parents 'phoned the North Pole' to report her misbehaviour. In her presence they advised the big man of her latest misdemeanour and proposed a cancellation of her account with immediate effect. 'No, Santa!' she yelled towards the phone, 'I'll be good, I promise.' It worked! She behaved. And it goes to show that Santa doesn't really give gifts after all. He gives rewards – performance-related Christmas bonuses. This is not the overflow of Santa's generous heart. It's part of a parent-sponsored global conspiracy to keep kids moral.

And perhaps this is the part of the Santa story that sounds most like our views of God. We fear that basically God is a big old moralist. You probably know this song:

> *He's making a list*
> *And checking it twice*
> *Gonna find out who's naughty or nice*
> *Santa Claus is coming to town ...*
>
> *He knows when you are sleeping*
> *He knows when you're awake*
> *He knows when you've been bad or good*
> *So be good for goodness sake[5]*

Have you ever stopped to consider how creepy this is? I mean, is it a Christmas carol or the North Korean national anthem? Alright, I'll stop now. I'm only having fun – I don't really hate Santa. (I'm deadly serious about turkey – that stuff is poison – but Santa is cool.) Here's what I'm really concerned about: *many* people think that God is a Santa in the sky, a childish fairy tale, or a distant moralist.

Whenever I talk about the Christmas message, there will be some who think I'm doing a (slightly) grown-up version of the Santa story. Perhaps that's how you think of Christianity – that it's basically about fleeing the darkness and buying any old myth so long as it's comforting. Perhaps you think God is a distant dispenser of blessings and curses – 'making a list and checking it twice'.

But Christians don't believe in Santa in the sky. If that's who God is, make me an atheist. Who can be bothered with an invisible benefactor far away? Who can believe by screwing their eyes shut to the darkness and hoping against hope? Not me. Not Christians.

When Christians talk about God, we're not talking about wish-fulfilment. We're not talking about a light we hope exists *beyond* the darkness. We're talking about a Light that showed up *in* the darkness.

Isaiah finishes his famous Christmas passage by talking about the promised Light. It turns out that the Light is a Person:

> *For to us a child is born,*
> > *to us a son is given,*
> > *and the government will be on his shoulders.*
> *And he will be called*
> > *Wonderful Counsellor, Mighty God,*
> > *Everlasting Father, Prince of Peace.*

— Isaiah 9:6

For Isaiah, the Light is not a concept or a fairy story. The Light is a royal Child born into our darkness.

This is the ultimate assurance of Light, not a vague belief or a groundless myth. Here is a happening in history. It's a happening that *made* history, resetting the calendar to the year zero. The coming of Jesus birthed civilisations, literature, art, philosophy and science. This is nothing like Santa. And it's nothing like humanity's attempts to imagine God. Here is a Light from beyond who shows up personally in our midst. He can be investigated, and billions of people of different cultures, races and ages have been persuaded that he is trustworthy.

Santa gives rewards from a distance. Here is a Light who gives himself to us, radiating God's own presence and peace. Here is a Child who grows to be a man; a King who shoulders our burdens. According to the verse above, we can picture a gift tag hanging around his ankle. It reads, 'From: God. To: You.'

This is a very different prospect. It's our fourth kind of Christmas ...

4. STABLE

Come with me to the stable in Bethlehem. It's 700 years after Isaiah wrote and yet all his words are coming true:

> *[Mary] brought forth her firstborn son, and wrapped him in swaddling clothes, and laid him in a manger; because there was no room for them in the inn. (Luke 2:7, KJV)*

The scene feels so domestic, so 'ye olde', so traditional. In fact, it is the most astonishing revolution imaginable. Think of the heights and the depths contained in this stable.

The firstborn son, is of course, Jesus. He is the one Isaiah called 'a great light … Mighty God … Prince of Peace'! But what happens at this first Christmas? He participates in mammalian birth! He is born into the human race to become our *brother*. Born to Mary – an unmarried, dirt-poor teenager. Born into a suffering, subjugated people. Born, we suppose, into a stable – a cattle shed. He is laid in a manger – a feeding trough. And, if Isaiah's predictions have been correct, He's born to die – born to descend into the depths of our pit.

The traditional Christmas is utterly revolutionary. The King of heaven becomes powerless. The Light of the world descends to the darkness. The giver of life is born to die.

This is God's solution to the darkness. We might have responses to the world's brokenness but Christmas is *God's* answer. Here's how it works.

The Christmas Child is God's eternal Son, joining our race by the power of the Holy Spirit (Luke 1:35). This means he's not just a special baby; he's an eternal member of that divine family – the Trinity. For this reason Isaiah (and others) can call him the 'Mighty God'. He has always been in on that family of love – Father, *Son* and Holy Spirit.

But he didn't just bathe in that eternal light. In the stable he entered our darkness, because this is what love does.

Christmas-time sees airports crammed full of tearful reunions. People pay thousands and cross oceans just to be with one another. Why? Love bears the cost to draw near. And Jesus bore the cost to draw near to us. At Christmas, God the Son became God our brother, because love pays any price to be with the beloved.

Imagine you are at the airport waiting for your own Christmas reunion. Your successful older brother is flying in from New York. He's been living there for the last ten years while you have struggled on at home. Dad died six months ago, Mum's been diagnosed with Alzheimer's, you're out of work and the debts are piling up. He approaches with more bags than you expected and with tears he says, 'I'm back for good now. We'll get through this.' This is the meaning of Christmas. Jesus did not merely pay us a visit in the stable. God the Son became our elder brother. He joined himself to our family in all its poverty and he pledged his life to us forevermore. When you see Jesus in the manger, you're seeing a promise – he is committing himself to our race and to our plight. In the stable the Christmas Child, though speechless, is speaking volumes. Essentially he's saying, 'I'm here now. I have come to shoulder your burdens, just like Isaiah promised.'

As he grows up, Jesus' burden-bearing nature takes him all the way to the depths of the pit – all the way to godforsaken death. Christmas leads to the cross. There Jesus takes on himself our sins and all the judgement that they deserve. The cross shows just how far our elder brother goes to shoulder our burdens.

Love bears the cost, and on the cross Jesus bears the cost for all that separates us from God – paying off our debts to God in full. He suffers the dark hell which our sins deserve and then bursts through death and into life on Easter Sunday. Now he comes to each of us in this land of deep shadow and says, 'I know your darkness. Let me be your light.'

This is the ultimate Christmas gift. As Isaiah says, 'to us a son is given'. If you call out to Jesus, asking him into your life, you receive him as your own Lord and guide through the valley. He takes the government of your life on to his shoulders. He fills you with his Spirit so that his Spirit is now your Spirit. He introduces you to his Father so that his Father is now your Father. He promises you his future so that his eternal life is now your eternal life. It's all for free and that gift tag around his ankle is true: it's all FOR YOU. So how will you respond?

WHICH KIND OF
CHRISTMAS ARE YOU?

1. SCROOGE

A Scrooge says, 'Darkness wins, get used to it.'

→ But we know that we're built for joy.

2. SHOPPER

A Shopper says, 'Darkness is coming, so we'd better celebrate now.'

→ But we know that we're built for hope.

3. SANTA

A Santa says, 'Forget the darkness, all is light.'

→ But we can't deny the truth of our plight.

4. STABLE

The Stable says, 'Darkness is real, but the Light has dawned.'

→ Here we face the truth of our darkness yet joyfully hope in the light.

Where do you stand on Christmas? Where do you stand on life?

With Jesus, you get the best of the other three options. You can acknowledge the darkness, you can celebrate in hope and you can look to a God who is no fairy tale. He can be known and is *worth* knowing.

Look to the stable and see God's Word to you. That's how the most famous Christmas reading,

John chapter 1, describes Jesus. Jesus is 'the Word' of God (John 1:1). In other words, he is the communication of God (John 1:14). He is God-speaking-to-you. There, wriggling in the manger, is God's attitude towards you. He does not send a thunderbolt; he sends his Son. He does not want to be distant. He's not *watching* from heaven, waiting for you to put a step wrong. He does not ask you whether you've been a good boy or girl this year. He knows you at your worst and he loves you anyway. He comes, he stoops and he draws alongside us. Don't you just love Jesus?

If you find yourself answering, 'Yes', then maybe it's time you told him so. John's famous Christmas reading says this about Jesus:

He was in the world, and though the world was made through him, the world did not recognise him. He came to that which was his own, but his own did not receive him. Yet to all who did receive him, to those who believed in his name, he gave the right to become children of God ... (John 1:10–12)

If you want to respond to God's ultimate

Christmas gift, these verses tell you what to do. As you recognise Jesus for who he is, then you *receive* him into your life. When you do so, you gain Jesus as your Lord – he becomes your guide as well as your friend. You also are given his Spirit as your Spirit and his Father as your Father. You become a forgiven child of God forever.

Is this something you want? It will mean receiving a new direction in your life – Christ's. It will also mean entering God's extended family – the church. But this new direction and new community are exactly what you need as you walk with Jesus through the darkness and into the light.

Here is a sample prayer if you want to receive Jesus. The specific words aren't important but something like this might help you unwrap God's Christmas gift:

Dear Father,

It's hard in the dark. And I recognise that there's darkness in me too. I'm sorry for my selfishness and sin. Thank you for Jesus – your gift. Thank you that he came to live my life here in the darkness. Thank you that he died my death on the cross and thank you that he rose again. I now receive him into my life. May he be my Lord, my guide and my friend forever.

Accept me as your child, fill me with your Spirit and help me to walk with Jesus and his people through the darkness and into your eternal light.

In Jesus' name,

Amen

If you have prayed like this, tell a Christian friend and tell us at info@fourkindsofchristmas.com. We would love to connect you with other believers close by and help you to take those first few steps in the Christian life.

If you're not ready to pray yet or you're a Christian already, then please check out our website – www.fourkindsofchristmas.com – for more resources to get you thinking and sharing.

Whatever kind of Christmas you're having, may it be a blessed one. In your darkness, may you know his Light.

The people walking in darkness
have seen a great light;
on those living in the land of deep darkness
a light has dawned.
You have enlarged the nation
and increased their joy;
they rejoice before you
as people rejoice at the harvest,
as warriors rejoice
when dividing the plunder.
For as in the day of Midian's defeat,
you have shattered
the yoke that burdens them,
the bar across their shoulders,
the rod of their oppressor.
Every warrior's boot used in battle
and every garment rolled in blood
will be destined for burning,
will be fuel for the fire.
For to us a child is born,
to us a son is given,
and the government will be on his shoulders.
And he will be called
Wonderful Counsellor, Mighty God,
Everlasting Father, Prince of Peace.

— Isaiah 9:2–6

NOTES

1 Colin Buchanan, *Aussie Jingle Bells* (Universal Music, 1996). Lyrics printed with permission.

2 http://comres.co.uk/wp-content/themes/comres/poll/Theos_Christmas_Poll_Dec10.pdf

3 http://www.telegraph.co.uk/finance/jobs/11244398/Hate-work-Christmas-parties-Heres-why-it-might-still-be-worth-showing-up.html

4 T.S. Eliot, 'Burnt Norton' (1935), part of *The Four Quartets*.

5 'Santa Claus Is Coming to Town', written by J. Fred Coots and Haven Gillespie (1932).

10Publishing is the publishing house of **10ofThose**.
It is committed to producing quality Christian
resources that are biblical and accessible.

www.10ofthose.com is our online retail arm selling
thousands of quality books at discounted prices.

For information contact: **info@10ofthose.com**
or check out our website: **www.10ofthose.com**